The Girl From Brooklyn

To Annie
Best friends
life

Marie
2017

The Girl From Brooklyn

MY STORY OF LIVING WITH DEPRESSION

Maria Medina
Introduction by Kathy Granas PhD

This is a work of creative, autobiographical nonfiction. The events are portrayed to the best of Maria Medina's memory. While all the stories in this book are true, some names and identifying details have been changed to protect the privacy of the people involved.

The advice and strategies found within may not be suitable for every situation. This work is sold with the understanding that neither the author nor the publisher are held responsible for the results accrued from the advice in this book.

Dedication

This book is dedicated to Chase Van Horn, the son of Renee and Gary Van Horn.
December 18, 1986 - September 7, 2011

Contents

Acknowledgments

I want to thank Jesus Christ my Lord and Savior for making this book real. I want to acknowledge the importance in my life of Ramon Ernestina, my mother, Jose, Hector, George, Tony, Robert, Victor and William, my brothers. Victor, you are a special person - sister Maria.

Crystal - Please never give up! I love you very much, mom.

Friends who are important to me include: Deb Mahon, Lyn Sadler, Kathy Granas, Marla Frey, Sue Schneider, Renee Van Horn, Janine Funk, Debbie Allen, Nancy Gregg, Carol Myers, Jeannie Sundholm, Ann Clark, Katie Joseph, Kathy Danaher, Judy Houston, Linda Rogers, Pastor Richard, Pastor Mark Raskam, and Melissa.

People like Renee have read through my book and have made comments such as: "Maria! Proud of you! Sure looks like God has provided throughout your life! You make others feel good about themselves, a gift of encouragement!"

I want to emphasize Steve Baker's help to me with my car. He makes me feel like I am family. I am able to talk to him about cars, and he explains things to me and breaks it down in a way that makes me understand and have confidence. My car is my lifeline of transportation to get to work. It is so important to me.

I want to mention Joanne Baldwin. For the last year and a half she has been helping me with my depression. When I call Joanne to come over to my house, she comes over and spends time with me and we pray and we talk. She comes to my job and hangs out with me. That makes me very, very happy. She and her husband, Munson, really help me.

Renee Van Horn, Lyn, Carol Myers, and Deb Mahon always say to me "I am proud of you. Keep pushing forward!" That really boosts my confidence.

Today I still go to Rocky Church. The pastor's name is Pastor Jess Mahon. He is the senior pastor of Rocky Church. I go to River Place. That is a place where I can have coffee and talk to somebody if I want to. It is part of the church. River Place is a good support system.

There are so many people in Estes Park who have made a difference to my life.

At the State Farm office: Susan, Katie, Lilly, and Russell.

At the Credit Union Bank: Debbie, Barbara, Sandy, Chelsea, and Julie.

At Big O Tires: Will, Kathy, Serena, Joe, Wayne, Jessie, Kenny, and Cyrus.

At Kind Coffee: Amy.

At Radio Shack: Thank you, Garrett, for helping me with my phone.

At Safeway: Scott, Carey, Michelle, Debbie, and Tiffany.

My dentist: Dr. Daniel M. Rauk and his staff.

At the Estes Park Library: Diane, Maggie, Wendy, Peggy, Gretel, Claudine, Kathleen, Gina, Joanna, Katha, Terri, and Kurtis.

At Dad's laundry: Candy, Heidi, and Caroline. At the post office: Carol, Kenny, Terry, Patty, and Michelle.

At the YMCA: Melisa, the assistant Human Resources Director. Thank you, Melisa, for being a support system for me.

The owner of the newspaper has made a big difference. Her name is Kris Hazleton.

My neighbor, Stephanie, and also Gary and Celeste have been important friends to me.

I want to thank Chaplain Greg for helping me pay my June, 2016, rent.

I get so excited when my birthday comes around. Deb Mahon always makes a big deal about my birthday. We start talking about my birthday in September. My birthday is in November. I get so excited and happy that she is going to do something special for me for my birthday!

My brother, Robert, always has said to me "You keep that hope alive". That keeps the fire burning inside of me.

I want to thank Lyn Sadler, my therapist. I also want to thank Amber and Linda, both with the mental health services.

Crystal, I love you very much. I am very, very proud of you. Please, I beg you, when you have problems run to Jesus. Call on your therapist. But don't give up that fight. Keep pressing forward. Please don't give up. Love, your mother, Maria.

My desire is to build a handball court here in Estes Park for everyone to learn how to play. I want to thank the Rocky Mountain Health Club for their handball court. I have been the handball teacher there for the past 8 years. I want to thank all the players that I have taught. Kevin is a wonderful player. I knew that you had it in you, Kevin. You are the shark! I am so happy that you beat me because that means I am a good teacher. That gives me such joy. Justin, Mike, Michael, Doug, David - I want to thank you very much for allowing me to be your teacher. I want to continue to keep the game alive.

Jeannie, I will be your friend for life.

BK Brooklyn

Maria

Introduction

by Kathy Granas, PhD

want you, the reader, to be aware that Maria has written this book about her life as someone who does not have a high school diploma. That has made a big difference in her life. She has worked through many years of difficult times, struggling with mental health issues, bipolar disorder, and learning disabilities. She has had serious episodes of suicidal depression, frustration, fear, and anxiety. She has often struggled with anger, impatience, and a feeling that she is not in control. This has led to periods when she can't sleep or eat normally. She has cried more tears than she has ever thought possible. She continues to struggle. But she has hope.

She has written this book with the hope of sharing with anyone else who struggles with symptoms and issues such as hers that you don't need to give up. You must get help and you can get help and you will be able to keep going. She has dedicated this book to Chase Van Horn, the son of very dear friends of hers. Chase was 24 years old when he committed suicide. He struggled with many of the same mental health challenges that Maria has. She wishes she could have told Chase what she is trying to tell the reader in this book. Don't give up. It will get better.

There are resources available and coping skills that can be learned. There are medications available and there are mental health professionals who care and who can guide you to what can help you, individually. She has written this book about her life because that is what she knows. She also knows that her life is much better because she had the help of family, friends, and mental health professionals. She continues to struggle with challenges and episodes of anger and depression, of fear and anxiety. But because she has found people who care about her and know what is best to help her, Maria has confidence that she can keep going through tough times and that everything will be ok. She also has her faith, and that gives her a lot of courage and strength when she needs it.

As you read Maria's story, you will learn about Lyn, her mental health therapist. Lyn has taught Maria many coping skills to help her get through difficult times. Life is not easy for anyone. But sometimes little things can set Maria off. She is learning what to do when that happens. She continues to work with Lyn and continues to learn how to deal with difficult times and unexpected disappointments. Lyn has taught Maria coping skills such as mindfulness - staying in the here and now. She has taught her how to respond to impulses and to learn to think things through before she acts. Lyn has taught Maria how to ride out a storm and to know that it will pass, to keep to her routine and trust that there will eventually be sunshine again. Lyn has taught Maria how to learn to keep going forward and how to handle those roller coaster rides. Maria has learned how to challenge negative thoughts and how to block thoughts that are distracting or misleading. Lyn has taught Maria how to learn the difference between feelings and thoughts and how to better understand herself.

There are many different routes to finding what will help you since each of us is different. There is therapy, effective diagnosis by a qualified doctor, support groups, workbooks, medications, supervised and staffed gathering places with supported work and field trips, etc. This book is not meant to give advice to any reader except to encourage you to go forward. Don't step backwards and don't stop. Keep going and know that you will find people and resources that will help you.

Maria's life has not been easy. It still is not easy. But she has discovered that when she wants to do better for herself, people will help her. Somehow doors open and she finds herself on a path that leads to something better. That is what you will see when you read her story. If she can help one person realize that there is help available, then the purpose of her book has been fulfilled. Once you help one, you help many. Every time someone helps Maria, it makes her more determined to do things in her life that will help others.

Maria is not a writer. She is someone who has an important story to tell, and it is important because it has the possibility of helping someone who feels lost to realize that they don't have to stay lost. There are steps they can take. There are answers that will help. This book is proof that there are people who care about you. Maria cares about you.

Maria dictated this book, word for word. These are Maria's words. They may not be said smoothly as they might be if English had been her first language or if she had been more of a reader and a writer during her life. Hopefully you, the reader, can hear Maria's voice, her pain, her struggles, and her passions through her honest words that tell her story. This book that Maria has written comes from her heart. She wants to thank Jesus Christ, her savior, for all the help He has given her in making this book in hopes to help others.

CHAPTER 1

Early years

My full name is Maria Milagros Medina. This is my story. I want to include you so that maybe my successes can become your's. I have been blessed with a lot of help... here is my story.

My father named me Milagros, which means "miracle". That is because I had seven brothers, Jose, Hector, George, Tony, Robert, Victor, and William. My father was in shock that I was a girl.

I was born in Brooklyn at the Coney Island Hospital, November 15, 1967. My mother and my father, they both were born in Puerto Rico. Puerto Rico is part of the United States, it is not a country. Two of my brothers were born in Puerto Rico.

My father got his high school diploma in Puerto Rico, and he went to two years of college in Puerto Rico. His goal was to be a college professor. He learned English in school in Puerto Rico. He taught himself to understand English better by reading books. He was always reading and learning. He also learned English better by always reading the New York Post every morning. He always had a dictionary next to him. If he didn't know a word, he would always look it up and sound it out.

My father had come from a family of 5 children in Puerto Rico. His parents had adopted a 6th child, Juan, because Juan's mother couldn't take care of him. She just didn't have the money to take care of Juan. When my father was 17, his father died of gangrene due to poor medical conditions in Puerto Rico. My father saw his father suffer. Because of my father's father dying when my father was 17, my father learned everything from his mother. She taught him to cook and to sew.

My father met my mother when they were around 15. They lived in a small village. My father had 3 sisters and 2 brothers. My mother had 4 sisters and 3 brothers. Both families grew up on farms, where big families were helpful to have. Spanish people don't believe in nursing homes. They have lots of children because when the parents get older it will be the children's responsibility to take the parents into their home and take care of them. The parents are never a burden to their children. That is how it is. My parents got married when they were 18.

My father, Juan Ramon Medina, and my mother, Ernestina Medina, they both moved to Brooklyn, a borough of New York City, in the late 1950s. My father wanted to have a better life for his family and felt like moving to New York would give him that opportunity. My mother knew no English. It took a lot of courage to make that move.

In Brooklyn when they still had just two boys, Jose and Hector, my father signed up for the army. He went to Vietnam during the war. He was a soldier. There were times during battles when he used his sewing skills that his mother had taught him to help other soldiers who were wounded. Medics were not available and quick thinking was needed. My father was there. Later in life, my father would share stories of his war experiences as a way of working through what we call today, post traumatic stress.

He was a kind man, a good father, a loving father. He had a lot of courage. He worked as a maintenance man/porter for a company. He worked there until he retired. We always lived in good neighborhoods. We never lived in the projects. We always lived in white neighborhoods due to my father's skin color. He had light coloring in his skin. Many people thought he was Polish or Russian. But he was Puerto Rican.

I was very attached to my father. When he used to start to go to work, I would hold on to his pants and try to keep him home. He explained to me that he needed to work to provide for his family. But that showed how much I really was attached to him. He gave me a sense of security. God provided a father for me who was an example of hard work, courage, bettering oneself, and resourcefulness.

When my brother, Robert, was 14 years old, my father would take us to the park on weekends. He loved to do that. He enjoyed interacting with his kids. He would hit the baseball and watch us run for it. One time my brother, Robert, was running and all of a sudden he had an asthma attack and started to fall. My father immediately caught Robert and rushed him to the hospital. I will never forget my father saving Robert. He was such a generous and godly man.

My mother was not so nice. She was a little bit cold. That might have had something to do with the way my mother's mother had treated her. My mother's mother was cold. She barely smiled. She was never friendly. She was always critical. She would put my mother down for no reason. My brothers didn't want to be around her because she was critical. They loved being with my father's mother but they didn't want to be around my mother's mother.

My grandmother would physically hit my mother with a broomstick when she was a teenager. Her sisters protected her from her mother. They would physically stand in the way to protect her. I think my grandmother's physical abuse might have impacted my mother's brain. When it came to me as her daughter, she wasn't nurturing. She was not there for me.

Growing up, my father did everything. He cooked for us. He sewed our clothes. He suspected my mother had some mental problems. She might have been bipolar. She started showing symptoms by spending money foolishly and impulsively. She would not be home on time. She would go somewhere and forget her way back. Fortunately, the neighborhood we were living in understood the situation. The neighbors would help my mother. God provided community for me. People that cared about us would make sure that we were taken care while my mother was out. My father just prayed to God that he could hold the family together.

My brothers, Victor and William, and I had learning disabilities. We had trouble learning English. We had trouble learning to read, write, and do math. We had trouble learning everything. It was very hard for us to be in school. I remember the three of us struggling so hard. My father saw the reality of this but he was determined to love his family, no matter what. He just kept us moving forward by encouraging us and being persistent.

My father taught us to read. He would get books to help us learn words in English. The schools in our neighborhood were not so good. They kept teaching the Puerto Rican kids in Spanish, and that is not what we needed. But my father was determined to help us with school and he would work with us until 10:00 at night, every day. On the weekends, he would take us out to the park. He taught me a good balance of hard work and play.

I was blessed because I did have two outstanding teachers. I passed the sixth grade because of my teacher, Sharon Wise, she cared about me. She more than helped me. She worked with me on my reading day after day. There was a teacher, Ann, my fourth grade teacher, she also helped me. Not just help. She cared. She cared about the whole family and me. She did more than just her job. Her caring was remarkable. She would knock on students' doors to get them to come to school. Both teachers gave us students their phone numbers. God knew I needed these women because of my mom's absence.

My mother was living with us. But emotionally she was not there. Almost checking out. She let my father do all the work, all the cleaning, all the cooking, and all the taking care of the children. Sometimes she would go do the shopping when my father told her what we needed. I honestly think that I block out a lot of what my mother did when I was a child because it is too painful to remember.

What did help my mother was that her friend, Blanca, told her about church. My mother got involved with the Spanish Pentecostal church. She became a different person because of that church. She got more involved with us children. Blanca was teaching her that she needed to love all of her children. Blanca was a good example to my mother of how a mother needed to be. Now when my father would take us to the park on Saturday, she would come with us. She started taking us children to church with her, as a family.

There were times, however, that my mother gave more attention to my brothers, especially Robert and Tony. I felt some rejection because of this. My father would get angry with her when she didn't give me as much attention. One time I fell off my bike and hurt my hand badly. My mother didn't seem to care. I still have the scar on my hand today because she didn't take care of it right away. My father and other friends from church would tell her that it was not just her sons but that she needed to care about me, too. Maybe my mother had modeled what her mother had done with her, not give attention when it was needed. Today I think my mother regrets that she didn't show me more affection. She made up for all of the times she was not there for me by being there for Crystal, my daughter.

CHAPTER 2

Growing up in Brooklyn

When I was 9 years old I went to Salem Church because the neighbors had told us that they had free activities for kids, free lunches, and Bible classes. Salem Church had a Bible club. Kathy was the leader of the Bible club and she lived in Brooklyn. She was a mother-like figure. She was caring. I noticed that when I was little and received attention from a mother-like figure, that was really important to me. Kathy impacted my life in a special way because she was what I wanted in a mother. She was kind and she was interested in me.

Kathy was my anchor for 3 years. She was my refuge. I felt secure with Kathy's friendship and help. But then Kathy got married and moved to New Jersey. She left my life. I lost my refuge and my anchor.

When Kathy left the role of being the Bible Club leader, Salem Church needed a replacement. Jennifer was the replacement. She was a teacher and she played the guitar. Kathy had just been the Bible Club leader. Now Jennifer took over that role. Now I was 12 years old and Jennifer came into my life.

I was held back three times in the seventh grade. I came home and told my father I just couldn't do it anymore. I couldn't learn anything. It was 1980 and Jennifer had come into my life. Jennifer was white. She said hello to me and I said hi back. With that hi back, we got involved. She wanted to learn more about me. I wasn't able to tell her much since I didn't know that much English. I told her where I lived and that if she wanted to meet my father and my mother she could. She went and met my parents and asked them if she could be a part of my life. Jennifer wanted to be like a mother to me, she was not married and had no kids. My father said that it would be ok if she wanted to be more involved in my life.

Jennifer put me into Salem Christian Academy. She paid for me to go to school and for me to learn something. I could walk to the Salem school. Pastor Marty Hagland was the principal of the school. And his wife, Evelyn was one of the teachers who helped give me attention at school during the day.

At that time Jennifer had no husband and no children. She saw helping me as a chance to help give to someone. She was a good teacher, a great teacher. Jennifer was like a mother to me. She was the one who would go to parent conferences for me and with me. She took me to the doctor's. She took me to church. She took me to the Bible Club at 7:30 pm on Fridays. I didn't know that much English. She would help me with my school work, she would read the Bible with me, take me to doctor and dentist appointments. She would help me pick out clothes and help me learn how to dress like a girl, not a tomboy. She was helping me to have a stable life.

My parents and my brothers were so happy that Jennifer was helping me grow up. My brothers were very protective of me, I was blessed that way. They were so happy to see a motherly person, like Jennifer, helping me. I wanted to live with Jennifer. I loved my family, but I was wanting to have stability and consistency in my life. That's what Jennifer was teaching me. It felt good when she would take me to a doctor's appointment when I was sick because it felt like she really cared and it made me feel safe.

I was glad to be with Jennifer because she could speak English and she was all about education. That was important to me because education was how I knew I could make it in this life.

However, things started to change. Jennifer made a friend at work and started doing some things without me. All of a sudden there were times when she didn't want me to do things with her. Whenever Jennifer got tired of me, she would just send me home. It felt like she only wanted me around when it was convenient for her. That is when confusion started building up in me. She gave me a lot of attention when I was 12 and 13. But when I was 14 it felt like things were changing.

When I was 14 I met Sue Schneider. She was incredible. Sue was teaching the kindergarten children. She invited me to her youth group and sh was one of the leaders of the youth group. She would take me everywhere with her. I would go to her house a lot. We were very close and were good friends. She was very kind. God really blessed me with a lot of good people. At times, I felt somewhat rejected by Jennifer. Sue didn't care if I was with her 24 hours a day, 7 days a week. Sue made me feel like I was her sister. We would do fun things together and activities. It felt like Sue really enjoyed my company more than Jennifer did. Jennifer needed us to plan things. Sue was spontaneous and enjoyed life! This was confusing to me because Jennifer and Sue each treated me differently.

I also was still playing handball. I had started playing handball when I met Jennifer because of the neighborhood where I was living. I was 12 when I started playing handball. All the kids either played handball or basketball at the park where it was free. Juan taught me how to play handball. He was Puerto Rican, too. I loved the game. I played 6 days a week. I would play from 4 pm until 7:30 pm. Handball was and still is a great gift from God that continues to bless me today. I love handball because it is a challenge. It makes me work hard. It is in my blood. It is a passion of mine. I am good at it.

I also went to a youth group, starting when I was 14. I loved youth group. It was through the First Evangelical Free Church. I had good friends at youth group. We were always having fun. That is where I met Annie Mahany and Diane Michiagno. They were really good friends. I had so much fun with them. They were a positive influence on me. They were into studying the Bible like I was. They weren't into drinking or drugs. They just wanted to have good, clean fun. They were interested in helping other people. I am still friends with Annie today. Annie had a good mother. I saw how Annie's mother was nurturing. That is what I wanted. Annie had a good education and that is what I wanted. Annie was always looking out for me like thinking about jobs I might have in the future. I admired how she went to school full-time and also had a part-time job. Diane finished high school, too. That was a goal I had. I was lacking education big-time and wanted to better myself.

My father started going to the Spanish Pentecostal church when I was 15. This was the same church that my mother was going to. The pastor was Pastor Felipe. My father had known Pastor Felipe for at least 40 years from knowing each other Puerto Rico. Pastor Felipe's wife's name was Grisel. God gave me continuous examples of the positive role a church can play. That church was important because that church prayed for me a lot. That is the way of the Pentecostal church. The pastor makes a list of whose house the congregation is going to focus on each week. Then the congregation comes to that person's house for several hours in the evening. They sing songs, they pray, they bring cake and food. They ask for testimonials about what God is doing in their life. They ask for people's struggles and they help lift them up. The pastor's wife would come to our house a lot and pray for the whole family. She nurtured my mother to be a better mother. She would help my mother know what she might do to help us more. My father was ordained to be the deacon of that church. He was in charge of the singing and the Bible study. The church was very important to us. My mother and father believed in Jesus Christ, and they raised us to do that, too.

I got a job at Nathan's Famous Hot Dogs when I was 16. I worked there 3 1/2 years. I took orders. It was a great experience. It was a lot of fun and it helped my father with money. It meant I could buy my own things like shoes, clothes, personal needs and not depend on him. Work has always been a positive thing in my life. I worked at Nathan's from 12 noon until 8 at night on Saturdays. On school days I worked 5 pm till 8. Sundays I went to church. When I wasn't working at Nathan's I would play handball. Sometimes I would play 5 games straight. I was very good.

I stayed in the Christian school until 1987. The school didn't have grades. You learned at the pace that you needed. I stayed in school until I was 18. Then I got too old for the school, so I left. I never got my high school diploma.

I was 18 and I met Paul at youth group. It was like love at first sight. He was Norwegian and I was Puerto Rican. There were a lot of Norwegians in Brooklyn. We were so much in love with each other. He was not honest with his mother. She didn't like him to date anyone who wasn't Norwegian. So I didn't know where I stood. Here again I was feeling rejection and confusion. Are we good or are we not good? Again there was no consistency. I felt like I was hanging. And yet I was blessed to know that a good love like I had felt was possible.

When I would have these experiences of confusion and insecurity, it really affected my sense of trust. I was having trouble trusting because I was not sure when something would stay the same and when something might change.

Annie, my friend in youth group, was very smart. She went to college. One of her courses was to be an exchange student. She went to London. She met a man named Jason King. I don't know how it came up, but she told me to go to London. I said okay. I did it for her, but then again I did it for me. I was hurt because Paul and I were not going to be a couple. I had to face reality. I was not Norwegian. That was the first time I experienced racial prejudice. I was disappointed because his mom was a Christian woman and I was a Christian. But she still didn't accept me.

So I got a passport. I was 19. I was working at Blue Cross and Blue Shield, and my job was to file claims. I flew to London and got off at Heathrow Airport. It was a huge deal when I landed. I was waiting at customs and I was scared. My heart was beating. I was in London and this was a big deal. I was excited and scared at the same time.

Annie's boyfriend, Jason King, picked me up at the airport and showed me around for a little more than a week. Annie wasn't there at the time. I went there because Annie encouraged me to take a trip to meet her boyfriend. This was a good chance for me to just get away for a while. Then I went back to Brooklyn.

CHAPTER 3
Starting a family

Not too much later after that I met David, at a bus stop in Brooklyn in 1990. He was a knock-out! He was good looking and handsome. He approached me first which made me feel special. We started going out. He was kind. He was born in Canada and his parents moved to Brooklyn. He said he was going to stay with his parents in Brooklyn and find work. He was an iron worker. On our first date we went to see the movie, Goodfellas. I was working at an A & P supermarket in the bakery department. The reason why I had gone to the bus stop was that I was attending a course to better learn English. I always wanted to learn and to better myself. I wasn't happy with the fact that I didn't have a high school diploma. I felt like I was robbed and that something was missing in my life. It meant that I didn't have the option to go to college and to get a good job. It was like the door was closed for me. I wanted in.

David and I got married April 4, 1992. Pastor Robert Sundholm married us at the First Evangelical Free Church. That is where my youth group was and so I decided to get married there. I became very close to Pastor Rob and his wife, Jeannie. God blessed me with a lot of good people in my life. Our marriage was going good. David was going to church and met Jim Maxwell. Jim Maxwell was like a spiritual father to David, a positive influence. David's father had been an alcoholic. Jim was a godly man and modeled spiritual guidance for David. He was an important man in our lives.

David and I were doing a lot of activities from church. However maybe his depression got the best of him and he turned to drinking. He had been drinking since he was 14. He wanted to change but he just didn't know how. Maybe that was one of the things that attracted him to me. He had never met someone who was always going to church and not drinking. That was how I was. But it was too hard for him to change. I didn't know that he was an alcoholic when I met him. He hid it very well. He made a lot of money at his job. He used it for alcohol and drugs. It was so sad.

A good part of our marriage was our daughter, Crystal. Crystal was born in 1993. When she was born, David had been and was still in rehab. I think that knowing that he was going to be a father overwhelmed him. Deep down in his heart it was like he was fighting a demon. He couldn't even take care of himself. How could he be a father? I needed security and stability for my daughter. So I moved in with my parents when Crystal was about two months old. Living with my parents was a happy thing because it was security. My parents were about church and Jesus and not about drinking. I knew that I was in a good place.

David came out of rehab a few months later. He was working and he was living with my parents and me for a little while. Jim Maxwell mentioned to us about a ministry in the woods in Pennsylvania that would be helpful to David. It was a very helpful place for David. It was called Skyview Ministry. David got his high school diploma there. The counseling there was helping him learn how to be a better father and a better person.

I went out to visit David at the ministry. There I met Marla and her family. Marla and her husband, Todd, were involved in this ministry that was helping men who were involved with drugs and alcohol addiction. They were helping David with his problem. Marla became friends with Crystal and me. She welcomed us as if we were part of her family. She told me that I could come for the weekends and holidays. She offered us a refuge, and I needed that and I needed her nurturing. She helped me with Crystal and was only one phone call away always. When Thanksgiving came, I enjoyed being with their family. I felt welcomed and felt like I belonged.

I had to eventually apply for welfare, food stamps, medicaid, the works. David was not working and he was not supporting Crystal and me. I never knew when he was going to be helping me. When Crystal was around 3 years old, David was getting back into his old ways. He went back to Brooklyn and started drinking and doing drugs again. He ended up in jail for a year. It made me very sad that David chose alcohol over his family. It caused me a lot of pain.

At this point I kind of gave up on the marriage. I couldn't risk any more let downs, now that I had a child. I felt like David abandoned Crystal and me. I wasn't working. I was trying to figure out what was going to happen with my life. I started back to work, as a cashier at the Food City supermarket, to try to get my self esteem back.

All through this time, Sue Schneider had never left me as a friend. Sue helped me get back on track. She wanted to help me sit down and work out a plan. She was like my support system. She would pray with me. She was there for me if I needed help. She watched Crystal for me and babysat for me. She was very attached to Crystal and took her to the museum and did fun things with her.

CHAPTER 4

Depression enters my life

However, as time went on, it got harder and harder for me to hold it together. I began more and more to not feel like myself. I was having racing thoughts, lack of energy, no interest in playing handball. I couldn't sleep, I was always worried. I had all the symptoms of depression but I didn't know I was depressed. I didn't know how to get out of this feeling I was having. I learned that my father, when he had come out of the army, had dealt with depression and some post-traumatic stress disorder. I also learned that my father's sister and her daughter had struggled with depression and bipolar disorder.

Then I went to this place called Heart Share. They had counseling there. I met Patricia. She worked with me as a counselor since I was having suicidal thoughts. I would wake up and not remember where I was and who I was. Patricia told me that I had a nervous breakdown. She said I had to come with her or she would call the police. She did not think I was safe. Patricia put me in Lutheran Hospital in Brooklyn. They had a mental illness unit and I was not myself. I was depressed. My brain just couldn't function anymore. I had put my heart and energy into David. At this time, David was stable. He had his own apartment now, but he didn't want to have anything to do with Crystal and me. While I was in the hospital, my parents took care of Crystal. Sue was still a friend, but she was not a counselor, she didn't have the skills to help me, and she had her own life.

In the hospital they gave me psychiatric treatment, trying to find out the reason I couldn't function. Trying to figure out why I didn't want to continue living. That was the best thing for me, going to the hospital. I didn't want to live and I felt there was no hope for me. The hospital gave me what I really needed. I was in the hospital for a week. After that I stayed with my parents and continued to get psychiatric treatment as an out-patient. Patricia was my counselor. Patricia stayed with me and she continued helping me. I saw Patricia through Heart Share for two years.

After two years she transferred me to another outpatient facility and I worked with Don, a therapist. He really worked hard with me for two-and-a-half years. He wanted to help me get on my own a little more. Before I left Don, the judge ordered me to have social security disability. I just couldn't function with life. I got that because I really needed the extra help.

I just wanted so badly to have a better life. I could just taste it: to have a stable and happy life. I was glad that God gave me that drive, but I couldn't grab it. Lack of education and my depression made me crippled. During those years, I went through a lot of ups and downs every day. I would be fine for 2 hours and after that I would be crying or just laying down. During that time I couldn't sleep much. I was worried about Crystal. I didn't know how I was going to get through life. I wasn't working, I wasn't playing handball, and David wasn't helping me at all. Through the clinic, they helped me get a divorce. At that time David started seeing a woman, and soon after that he got married to her.

I hardly ever smiled and I was not happy. I was struggling with suicidal thoughts because I just didn't want to live any more. There was a lot of mental pain. I couldn't keep living with the mental pain. The mental pain was very dangerous. It was like you were on the bottom of the ocean and you wanted to come up and something is pulling you down. The people that helped me were Sue, Nancy, Jeannie, Pastor Rob, and my father's church. But the depression was too strong. It was so dark. My life had no light, and I felt no hope. It was terrible, like a nightmare. Nothing helped. Even going to church didn't help.

My parents felt helpless. They didn't know what to do. Then my mother called 3 women to pray for me. They attended Bayridge Christian Church and they were good friends of my mother. When they were done praying, they told me that God would help me and I just needed to have faith. Right after that, things changed!

That glimpse of faith helped me a lot. It was like I could see a light that God was shining. I went to a new church near my house. It was called Victory Outreach. I had been told that people at this church would pray for me. After those women had prayed for me, my tiny faith started to grow stronger and stronger. At the new church I met Karen. Karen told me that maybe I should move out of Brooklyn. She was saying that maybe the city was way too big for me. Maybe I needed a smaller place, like a pond instead of an ocean. I needed a bigger support system to help me get on my own instead of depending on and living with my parents. It was their castle, and I wanted my own castle. I didn't have any control.

CHAPTER 5
Moving to Colorado

So I decided to move. I felt like I had no choice. I wanted to have a better life. Karen's uncle told me of a place called Harvest House in Estes Park, Colorado that took women and children. So that is where Crystal and I could go. In 2003 I left Brooklyn and came to Estes Park, CO. My father, 9-year-old Crystal, 3 pieces of luggage, and I came to Colorado on a Greyhound bus. I came to Estes Park with a hope and a dream for a better life, for a chance to be happy. When I arrived, my faith was all in Jesus. I knew that this was what He wanted for me. I was not scared or worried at all. Being in Estes Park reminded me of being in the woods of Pennsylvania when I was 16 and I worked at Camp Hebron. This was not my first time being out of the city, and I felt like I belonged in Estes Park.

The Harvest House director, Sharon, came to pick us up at the bus station in Denver. I stayed at the Harvest House and I started to get a little better in handling myself. After a while, when my father saw that I was going to be ok, and he felt secure in leaving me at Harvest House, he went back to Brooklyn. This felt like I was getting a fresh start at a new beginning. At Harvest House, they helped me to be a better mother. They taught me skills of how to discipline Crystal and how to help her steer her in the right direction. Crystal was only 9-years-old and could barely read and write. They helped to home-school her.

The people at Harvest House were helping me. Just being out of the city in the small town of Estes Park helped bring a calmness to me. They helped me get a job at the Lake Shore Lodge in the laundry, and they gave me transportation to get to work. Crystal and I stayed in Harvest House for 10 months.

My move to Estes Park was a great move, and I had nothing to lose. I missed my family, but it brought a lot of peace to me to be in Estes Park. When I got to Estes Park, there was a calmness in my heart. I slept. I had no worries. I felt like God wanted me to be here, and whatever it took He was going to make me be here.

After ten months at Harvest House, my father wanted Crystal and me to have our own place. So I left Harvest House after being there for ten months. Soon after that I connected with Lyn Sadler, a therapist from the mental health services. I was honest and told her that I had been in a mental hospital and had to have medication. Lyn requested my chart from my old clinic and she didn't waste any time at all in helping me. This was in 2004.

We were living in Estes Park and Crystal was 10 years old. Judy Houston was working at Starbucks at that time. Crystal went right up to Judy and asked if she could take her to church. Judy asked Crystal where her mom was. Crystal brought Judy to meet me. I was working seven days a week at the time and couldn't attend church. So Judy began taking Crystal to church. We became friends. Judy never judged me. She only wanted me to be successful. She was always there for me, just a phone call away. She loved my company and loved hanging out with Crystal and me. I was making new friends.

I was out of Harvest House living on my own and I was working. But I needed help in providing the structure that Crystal needed. Crystal was only 10 years old but she wouldn't listen to me and she was just out of control. Crystal was going to school, but I didn't know how to help her. Lois Weaver, a friend from church, came into my life and helped me with Crystal. She helped Crystal go to a place in Longmont where she could live and go to school. It was like a farm with chores and it was a Christian place. Crystal would go to school and church, and she was involved in 4-H. This was a great place of stability and security for Crystal.

CHAPTER 6
New struggles

met Jeff in October of 2004. On February 9th, 2005 we got married. That was a mistake. The truth was I was lonely. I didn't really get to know him well. I didn't know it then but I had to be careful about what I did. With mental illness, you really have to be honest with your therapist and to let them guide you every step. Jeff was playing this role about being perfect: attending church, cooking for Crystal and me. But I really didn't know him enough. I didn't know about his drinking problem. He had hid it from me. But then he stopped going to church and his true colors came out. He started drinking a lot and became less kind. He started getting into his own world, and then again he would lash out at me. Drinking changes people. Within that first year of marriage his drinking became so bad that I had to go back to my family in Brooklyn for a month because I had to regroup. I had to figure out what would be best for me.

Going back to Brooklyn brought back bad memories for me. Memories can bring a lot of pain. I came back to Estes Park because I needed to be here for Crystal and for myself. While Crystal was staying at the place in Longmont, I would go to see her three or four times a week. Linda, one of her house parents, would bring Crystal to Estes Park to be with me on the weekends. I got an apartment and lived there for seven years. It was hard for me because Crystal was not living with me during the week. I had to adjust. But she was in a place that was helping her. My father had seen the place in Longmont and thought it was a good place for Crystal. That was a wonderful place for Crystal. She had structure and a routine. That was great for her since I had not been able to give that to her. We were both proud at her 8th-grade graduation because school for Crystal was really a challenge.

Crystal came back to Estes Park to live with me after 8th grade. (Jeff was still living with us because it was cheaper that way, but he wasn't involved with Crystal or me.)

The Longmont school, Mead, only went to the 8th grade. She went to public school in Estes Park for high school. That was very hard because it was not a very structured environment there. They didn't have what Crystal needed. They didn't have the special classes or the one-on-one help that she needed. She started running with the "wolf pack" and she got in trouble. The change from Longmont was very hard for her. It had been her decision to make that change to come back to Estes Park, but it wasn't a good decision.

Not too long after moving to Estes Park, she got in trouble with the police for stealing and for missing school. At 15 years of age, she was going to see Judge Beranado. I had no car. I didn't know how I was going to go to Ft. Collins to see the judge without a car. I prayed at church that God would help me. I saw Vicki, and Vicki said that she would help me with whatever I needed. Vicki drove us to Ft. Collins for all of the appointments from the court and all of the meetings we had to attend. She spoke for me. I learned how to speak and how to stand up for myself and for Crystal. Then Crystal didn't want to go to school in Estes Park. So the judge ordered Crystal to go to a school in Ft. Collins. The court paid for it. The school was called Turning Point. Crystal got a lot of help there because it was usually one-on-one help with a teacher. The staff from Turning Point would drive up to Estes Park every day and pick her up and take her to school and bring her home after school. Social services paid for Crystal's education because the judge was fighting for Crystal to have a better life.

When I finally stood up and told the judge that I didn't have a car to make that drive 3 times a week and that Vicki was driving me every time, the judge ordered social services to help me get my driver's license. In 2009 I got my driver's license. The man who helped me to get my license was named John. Pastor Richard in church gave me a car when I got my license. It was a 1995 Caravan minivan. That was my first car. I had gotten my drivers license when I was 19 in Brooklyn. But when is in the mental hospital, my license expired.

Crystal went to Turning Point for a little over a year, then the social services money ran out. She tried to go back to the Estes Park high school, but it didn't work out because they didn't have any special programs for students like Crystal who have bipolar issues and other learning disabilities that she had been diagnosed with when she was in Longmont.

Lyn, my therapist, stepped in and started working with me to help me be a better parent. I got Crystal a therapist through the mental health clinic after she had tried to hurt herself. She was also diagnosed with depression as well. This was a very hard time for both of us since we were both struggling with depression.

Lyn was always consistent with her support of me. I wasn't working. I wanted to have a job. I once again began to struggle after my car died after 4 years. I kept having hand-me-down cars, and it was frustrating that I had continuous problems with them.

All through this, Jeff and I were still living together. But he distanced himself emotionally and mentally. He wasn't helping me at all. This showed that he didn't really care about Crystal and me any more. We were not important to him. He was not reliable. We couldn't depend on him. One day he would be drinking and the next day he wouldn't. He was up and down with his emotions. He was working, but he was in his own little world. He didn't want to buy food for Crystal and me. He became like a monster. He was emotionally and mentally unstable. He was like Jekyll and Hyde, always changing.

I had to depend on God and pray a lot. I had to get on my knees a lot, and ask the people at church to help me. I felt alone. Jeff was there, but he wasn't there. I had to stay with him because I didn't have any money. I was stuck. How could I get my life on track again?

Finally I got a job at the Holiday Inn working in the laundry. I still had my social security check coming in, but that was not enough money for me to have my own place. I did not have long-term stability financially.

CHAPTER 7

Trying to keep going

In 2007 I had connected with Rocky church. In 2011 I asked Deb Mahon, the pastor's wife, to help me learn how to read better. Deb also helped me with dealing with my relationship with Jennifer. I had been thinking of Jennifer as my mother. She was the lady in Brooklyn who paid for me to go to Salem Christian School. But Deb helped me realize that a mother does not act like Jennifer had acted. That really helped me let go of seeing Jennifer as a mother, but instead just as a friend. That really freed me. When I was young, Jennifer was there for me and acted as a mother. When I got older, maybe she didn't want me to see her as a mother any more. I became confused. I do better with consistency. I didn't know that I was no longer part of her family any more. She was not coming to see me in Estes Park. I felt rejection and abandoned by her. That is when Deb Mahon helped me to build my self-esteem. The love that Deb Mahon had for me and the help that Lyn gave me helped me realize that I was going to be ok on my own. I didn't need Jennifer's approval any more.

In 2011 things once again became difficult. Crystal was in the mental hospital in Ft. Collins. She had gone through a really hard time and had taken a lot of dangerous pills. My car was in the shop and I had no transportation. I was frantic. Carol Myers from the post office came to my rescue by giving Big O tires her credit card so that I could get my car out of the shop and visit Crystal. Carol ended up helping me a lot, and I was very grateful.

Crystal finally was able to come home. I was so worried about her. Michelle was a therapist working with Crystal. Lyn was giving me the tools to help Crystal, but I didn't know what to do. I was afraid to leave her alone. I couldn't think straight. No mother wants to go through that. Life was not easy for me.

Crystal was very depressed and vulnerable and was thinking about killing herself. I was able to help her because I was a survivor of suicide attempts. I understood what she was going through. But as a mother I was scared and "walking on egg shells". No parent wants to go through that. I knew she was feeling hopeless and feeling an emptiness that nobody cared. I was able, with Lyn's help, to help Crystal get through this. Lyn kept on saying to keep pushing forward, that Crystal would learn from my example. I was Crystal's guide. It was a frightening time in both of our lives.

After Crystal came through that time, I wanted to share my story with the newspaper about mental illness and depression. I felt like there was hope for everyone. If I can get through these problems, so could they. I wanted to let them know that there was always hope and to please not kill yourself.

Crystal was working with Michelle, her therapist. I was nurturing Crystal to help build her self-esteem and to get to the root of her wanting to kill herself. I would reassure her every second that I was with her and that we would get through this together, things would be ok. I was wanting to be there for her. While I was doing that, Lyn was helping me. As time went on I began seeing Crystal get better and felt relieved.

My car, once again, was in the shop. For my birthday, Renee, a lady from church, paid the bill to get my car out. And Renee paid for my eye glasses. I looked at her as my hero. I didn't know how to thank her enough. God seemed to just take care of me with so many wonderful people throughout my life. Wonderful people like Renee, Carol, and Deb.

Debbie Allen I had known for 40 years since I lived in Brooklyn. She and her husband, Matt, were now living in Woodland Park, CO. She would come and pick Crystal and me up and take us to join them in Woodland Park for Thanksgiving and other holidays so that we would not be alone. We could be part of a family.

During this time, my father got sick in Brooklyn. My sister-in-law, Angelina, told me he was sick. I talked to my father on the phone and he told me that he was sick and that I needed to come to Brooklyn. Nancy Gregg from the church bought me a plane ticket. I went to my father and catered to him. I went to the doctor's with him at the VA hospital and learned he had colon cancer. I didn't know what to do and what to think. The thought of losing my father... My brother, Robert, used to call my father Superman, a man of steel.

My heart just sank when I saw my father so sick. I didn't know what to think. Somehow, someway I got strength and peace from God to remain calm. I asked the doctor where we stood and how long did he have. I didn't know that my father had been depressed and he hadn't been to the doctor's before.

My father had to go through chemotherapy. My brother, Victor, was very involved in helping take my father to the doctor. Victor was there a lot. My father had home care with Lou Maria. She catered to him. She did everything. She kept him company, she fed him, she bathed him. She tended to all his needs. At that time, I felt confident to leave my father. I told him that I would be back. My daughter also needed me.

When I got back to Estes Park I found everything different. Jeff had left our apartment because Crystal was out of control. When I had left to go back to Brooklyn, Crystal had started letting friends and anybody come over to the house. Jeff had to leave the apartment because of the disruptions. He didn't want to be held responsible if something went wrong in the apartment. When I got back from Brooklyn, Crystal and I needed a place to stay. The lady that owned the hostel in Estes Park, Terry, let me stay there for free with Crystal. Crystal got a job, and I hoped she would become more responsible.

I had told my father that I was coming back, and I did. I spent precious time with him. I knew in my heart that he was not going to live much longer. I was there for 2 or 3 weeks with my father. Then I came back to Estes Park, and Penny, a lady from church, let me stay at her house. After that, Jeff and I got a place because it was cheaper to split the rent. Crystal came back to live with us then. She had been living on her own since she had a job, but she just couldn't afford to keep having her own place.

I started praying to God to help me get a job. I told Lyn that I would love to work in the YMCA in the laundry department. That would be a good job for me. I had a big problem because of the car situation once again. There was no bus or train system in Estes Park and you needed a car. The cars that I had were hand-me-down cars. They always needed repairs. I had a Dodge Stratus, I had a Malibu, I had a Ford Taurus, I had an Infinity. They didn't last too long because they had so many problems and I couldn't afford to fix them.

I told Lyn that I didn't want to live like I was living any more. I wanted to prosper and have a better life. I wanted a job that was suitable for me, that I could stick with and that I could handle. I wanted a job that would make me have a better life. I needed Lyn to start preparing me to be successful and I was prepared to work for it.

CHAPTER 8

A more stable life

asked Deb Mahon if she could please help me get a job. All the job applications were online. Deb helped me apply online to get a job at the laundry at the YMCA. Linda Rogers hired me immediately. Soon after that Carol Myers helped me get a car loan so that I could have a reliable car. Debbie Delaney worked at the bank and helped me with that car loan. Without Carol Myers helping me to get the car, there was no way I could get the YMCA job. The YMCA was at least 5 miles from Estes Park. I called Steve, from the church, and he went online and helped me find my Subaru.

When I got hired for the laundry job at the YMCA, I was scared inside. I knew it was the right thing for me, and I had peace and happiness inside knowing that it was going to be ok. This was a life-changing experience for me. The job gave me more stability because I earned more money. I was able to pay bills. All of a sudden, I was able to have a job that would help me begin to help myself. Other people started helping me because they could see me begin to make changes in myself so that I could have a better life. I was proud of my accomplishments. I started planning to have my own place with Crystal and without Jeff. Jeff was drinking alcohol and that bothered me a lot due to my previous marriage. I got my job on August 20, 2013.

Then, sadly, my father died. My father died on December 7, 2014. Nancy Gregg bought tickets for Crystal and me to go back to Brooklyn for his service. Pastor Felipe was my father's pastor who gave the service at the funeral at the Spanish Pentecostal Church. My father wanted singing and a little preaching which is what there was. I spoke at the service and my brothers said something, too. Some of the people in the congregation spoke about how my father had changed their lives. My father was such a kind and generous man. People wanted to be around him. The youth group was at the funeral. He had encouraged them to stay in school and to keep going to church.

They loved my father very deeply. They enjoyed his company. They enjoyed my father a lot. My father was a great man. His death was a great loss, but it was comforting to see how he had touched many people's lives.

I am still working at the YMCA today. My happy days are when I am working there. It gives me a stability that I long for. I always look forward to going to work. I have part-time hours there. There are lots of people at the YMCA who have been and still are important to me. Rafael, Doug, Adam, Neil, Dennis, and Linda Rogers. They help me be successful on the job site. They all help me, especially when I have episodes. When you are struggling with depression, it is important to go immediately to your supervisor and tell them that you need support. Sometimes there are times when my brain is not working right, and they will take me aside and ask me what is wrong. They see that I am losing focus, and they encourage me to talk about it. When they help me talk about how I am feeling that gets me back on track. That helps me get through the day. When Rafael and Doug see me like that, they stop what they are doing and help me. They are sensitive, and they are right there for me at the moment. They always reassure me that it will be ok. When you have mental illness, please speak out and reach out and let people know that you are dealing with mental illness. They will help you.

Lyn, my therapist, and Deb Mahon, my pastor's wife, help me to have stability. They help me keep on pushing forward. They are my support system. I have learning from them coping skills that make me able to have a better life.

I still continue to have struggles in my life. In June, 2016 my social security check did not come. That was how I had been paying my rent. The judge ordered me to receive money from social security when I went into the mental hospital in Brooklyn. Ever since then the money helped me a lot to put a roof over my head.

Once a year I need to renew my social security disability situation. Every year, for the past 7 years, Lyn, my therapist would attach a letter about how important it was that I would get this money from social security. This year the social security people didn't read Lyn's letter. That is why they stopped sending the money. That really affected my life. I felt like I was going backwards in my mind. I lost my sense of security. I didn't want to live because I was frightened I would become homeless again.

Lyn kept on reassuring me that we were going to get through this together. Her reassurance was like a knock on the door letting me know that there was hope for me and she was going to fight the good fight with me. Amber, my case worker from the local mental health clinic, went with me to file an appeal to social security. Not too long after that, social security found Lyn's letter and read it. That is how they reopened my case and they said that they would start sending my social security money again. This was a relief. I felt at peace.

Fear is what I struggle with. My biggest fear is being homeless. I don't have family here in Estes Park. I have friends here. But when I am afraid and feel like I am all by myself, it is very hard. When I am afraid, I pray and I put my faith in Jesus. Jeremiah 17:7-8 says "Blessed is the man that trusteth in the Lord, and whose hope the Lord is. For he shall be as a tree planted by the waters, and that spreadeth out her roots by the river, and shall not see when heat cometh, but her leaf shall be green; and shall not be careful in the year of drought, neither shall cease from yielding fruit." Lyn's reassurance when I am feeling rejected is what makes the difference for me. I would not know what to do without Lyn and her support.

When you meet somebody like me that struggles with depression and mental illness, please give them a fighting chance. Give them all the encouragement they need. I work hard at my job at the YMCA. But I also work very hard to have a stable life and to be happy. Shame and guilt can kill. It took me a long time to accept the things in life that I cannot change. I had to admit that I did need the help from social security and from a mental health therapist.

CHAPTER 9

Have hope

I f you are struggling with depression, please, I ask you, don't wait any longer, not a second, not a moment. Go right away to your nearest mental health clinic. The symptoms of depression are emptiness, lack of energy, eating too much, not eating enough, racing thoughts, and a sense of hopelessness like nobody cares. If you are having suicidal thoughts, if you are hearing voices, if you get very angry or if you isolate yourself - these are all warning signs. If you are always crying about things that you shouldn't be crying about or if you take things the wrong way, you could be depressed. If you get irritable, that, too, is a sign of depression. Like me, I want you to get help. Don't spend one more moment debating. Get help immediately! When you reach out for help, you are free from the pain. There are people who can teach you coping skills that will help you get through the dark times. They will help work things out with you. Maybe you will need medication, too. There is nothing wrong with that. Medication can be very helpful.

When I was in Brooklyn, I had my family, I had Puerto Rican food, and I had the handball court close by. But I had no peace. The Bible verse, Jeremiah 33:3, spoke to me and let me know that God would provide. It says "Call to me and I will answer you and tell you great and unsearchable things you do not know." When I moved to Estes Park, I knew no one here. But whenever I asked God to help me, He answered me and that is what always got me through.

My mother and my father were married for 63 years. Their relationship was very strong because they both loved Jesus and they prayed a lot. They would go to church together and pray a lot. Today my mother is 85 years old. Her faith in God is very, very powerful. She always says to me, "Maria, when you have problems, you run to Jesus first and He will help you." My mother is very loving and caring towards me today. She is calling me to see if I need anything. She keeps encouraging me to push forward. We really miss each other and we have a good relationship today.

Handball has been so important to me. All of the school teachers I met really emphasized education. And education has become an important thing to me. But when I play handball, I feel like a winner. It is something I can teach to others. It really is important to me and I always want to be able to play. I do want to get my high school diploma, but handball has given me confidence all through my life. I started playing handball in Brooklyn when I was 12, and I kept on playing handball all through my life. In Estes Park I found Rocky Mountain Health Club. And for the past 8 years I have been coaching handball. I feel like a winner today in spite of my mental illness. If I can make a difference to myself and to others, then I am a winner today.

I want to be free from depending on other people all the time. I want to be self-sufficient and not be needy all the time. That is where Lyn and Deb have helped me start doing things on my own. I am very grateful that they have helped me build my self-confidence.

I am 48 years old today and I want to go back to school and get a high school diploma. There is so much more I want to do. Today I am a different person and you can be, too. Thank you for walking through my story with me.

Photos

Lyn Sadler with Maria

Deb Mahon with Maria

Crystal with Maria

Maria with Kris, the owner of the local newspaper

Maria, Kathy, Cyrus, Jeremiah, and Jessie
Friends at Big O Tires

Maria and Melissa, HR at YMCA

Maria and Jessica at Housing Authority

Maria and her coworkers at YMCA

Maria with Deb Mahon and Kathy Granas

Made in the USA
Charleston, SC
26 February 2017